When Queens Bridge the Gap

Author: Shenaé Pitts

Dedication

To the strong girls and women all over the universe…

"If I can uplift at least one little girl, one teenage girl trying to find herself, or a young woman coming into her own; we all win".

ISBN: 978-0-578-58330-3

CONTENTS

ACKNOWLEDGMENTS

To my mom and dad for having an influence on my life, but still allowing me to make mistakes, correct them, and grow from my experiences. To my late grandmother for helping to raise me into the powerful woman that I am today. To my best friend for always being there for me, even sometimes before herself. To my work family that turned into a group of lifelong friends. You pushed me to see the potential that I doubted within. To all of my family and friends who have genuinely supported my accomplishments and rooted me on every step of the way.

Happiness begins, or should begin, within. For me that meant understanding how to reach my happy place without hating or waiting on anyone. While on this journey, I found that the people who I chose to surround myself with crucially impacted my vibe and how I felt.

Thank you all, truly from the bottom of my heart. I would not have the confidence that I need to influence other women if it were not for you!

INTRODUCTION

Have you ever been ridiculed because of your age, race, or skin color? I'm most certain you have been, but nothing is stronger than the positive voices you choose to remember in those moments. I remember one scenario as if it were yesterday. One morning during elementary school a few of my classmates began to tease me and call me names. They laughed loudly, saying things like: "You're so black!" It didn't feel good. Furthermore, I didn't expect to receive negative vibes in an environment that should have been an emotionally safe place. In that moment I shrugged off the unwanted feelings and said to myself, *I'll be hanging out with my dad this weekend anyway, so all is well.*

● ● ●

Who or what is your safe place? Do you value the voices that speak over your life? My father was one of the voices that always reminded me that I was his beautiful, chocolate baby. My mother's voice allowed me to shrug off those negative words because her work ethic taught me how to keep it pushing.

I don't remember my mother complaining one bit about providing for me, because she had an ability to function well despite being under pressure.

Words impact us! The truth of the matter is that we're not fighting with skin tone or how much we weigh first. Our lifelong battles are spent fighting with how other people make and made us feel.

Now let's be honest – we don't start life out with a queen's crown, but rather someone places a princess's tiara on our head. We accept whether or not we have worth and value based on the first community we're introduced to—our families.

I didn't know it at that time, but my first tiara was not a physical one. It was one that you couldn't buy with money. It was my family's expression of love that crowned me with the understanding that I had worth and value.

From One Queen To The Next...

CHAPTER ONE
WE'RE RAISING QUEENS RIGHT?

Growing up, it took some time to become comfortable with who I was and what I represented. I was a young, dark-skinned little girl who loved to play with my cousins, eat my grandmother's cooking, and go fishing with my dad. From elementary to middle school, I made friends easily and stayed active in a variety of sports, including: track and field, cheerleading, volleyball, and basketball. I liked school and excelled in most of my classes due to my drive and self-perseverance. I took pride in being recognized for my achievements. I was taught right from wrong, simple manners, to treat others how I wanted to be treated, and to respect my elders. I was grateful to have those values instilled in me at a young age, but that doesn't mean I wasn't rebellious as a teen.

My mom and I often bumped heads during my teenage years, because I wanted to learn things on my own while figuring out who I wanted to be. She taught me to be independent which has served me well, but during my phase of immaturity I saw it as a curse. My mother allowed me to make mistakes and learn from them. We sometimes like to "test the waters" just to see what all the hype is about. Well, I'm here to tell you – save your curiosity.

Looking back, I've always felt like something was missing. I felt like I couldn't be happy until somebody made me feel like I should be happy, instead of creating my own happiness within. This was a gap that needed closure and over the years I searched near and far for my bridge. Life has taught me that gaps can't be filled with a person or thing, but it's your mindset changing that ultimately changes you from within. Given the chance to go back in time I would have a conversation with the younger version of myself.

What would I say? I'm so glad you asked! It would be to understand the power of making good decisions and that things don't happen by accident but mainly by choice.

I would tell my younger self to disregard what I thought I knew and mentally prepare for my journey of life lessons.

Most importantly, I would emphasize the need to accept and appreciate the rejections which led me where I am today. I don't want to run past this because rejection can be an instrument of development and character if the family is intact. What does that mean? Imagine someone saying that your shoes were ugly and lame, but you come a family environment where you feel loved. You would care less about what the next person thought of you. That's why it's so important to speak life unto your loved ones especially kids because this world is cruel.

Fix Your Crown

Queening: The act of tastefully embracing your individuality, leading by example, and living as a muse.

Finding the beauty within has allowed me to radiate a confidence so fierce that my self-esteem tends to often overflow. This is not to boast or brag about how I feel about myself, but to share my journey with you on how I reached this peace. I'm here to share with you how I fix my crown even on my worst days, and to help you fix yours too, Queen. If I can uplift at least one little girl, one teenage girl trying to find herself, or a young woman coming into her own; we all win. Too often we become competitors of other women because insecurities won't allow us to be genuinely happy for one another. We sometimes choose to tear them down instead of lifting them up. We decide to spread the negative instead of supporting the positive.

One of the things that brings me joy is to see someone reaching for their dreams despite challenges that come with life. Do you know how powerful you are to the world? I am your biggest fan Queen, and you're winning not because you always get what you want but because you learned more about yourself as you persevered. I look at my generation today and try to be the difference. I want to help change the perception and rally around all young girls and women, and let them know that they are not alone.

CHAPTER TWO
FAMILY TIES

Family, environment, and stabilization play a huge part in the upbringing of a child, from a teen, and throughout adulthood. I am aware that other factors may also be important, but let's narrow down the drivers. Chances are, if you didn't have a stable environment or a loving family, your upbringing may have left a damaging imprint on you.

Now some may have different opinions, but I believe that the love of a mother and a father are equally important. Although I didn't have both parents in one home, I appreciate my parent's ability to successfully co-parent, which gave me chance at having not one, but two loving families.

How do we successfully create strong family ties that benefit everyone involved? I whole-heartedly believe that healthy expectations play a huge role when we have blended families. Meaning it's healthy to understand that if the mother and father are no longer together then we have to honestly assess what's best for our children. It's healthy not to make our children choose which parent to value based on our inability to stay together. How many times have we seen the mother not having access to her children because the father was upset about mom's relational choice to move on? Mothers can also disallow interaction with the father based on unresolved issues, and despite how frequent this happens the fact remains that our children are being impacted by choices that were beyond them. Understand there are some real reasons for separating and to go back into the environment with an abusive man or even a verbally abusive woman can make you vulnerable to more abuse.

Who is the advocate in your blended family situation? Is it your aunt, mom, grandmother or close friend? Advocates are important because if not then the only bridge to civil interactions with the other parent will be social services or Friends of the Court (which is necessary at times) but that shouldn't be where we start if at all possible. My parents were able to be civil and I'm thankful for the balance that it provided me; it allowed me to focus on just being a kid, and not the added stress that parents tend to go through when one parent is not pulling their weight with the child.

A mother should be there to help her daughter be the best version of herself, to help her embrace her beauty and her worth, and to be the classy example of the woman she wants her to become.

A father should to be the first man to show his little girl what real love is and how a man who loves her should treat her. This is important in a young girl's life, because you control the creation of a cycle – her looking for love and validation from every man she encounters. As parents, the goal should be to teach young girls to be *somebodies* instead of somebody's.

When the Love Is Missing…

What if there is no love? What if you grew up wondering if your mother ever loved you or if your father ever cared? What if you then had a child of your own and had to teach them how that love should feel?

I've had conversations with some of these women. Most are still broken while others have managed to put the pieces back together and move forward. The impact to their upbringing was so detrimental that talking about it now takes them to a place that they've vowed to never return, and I can understand.

There are women who are still struggling with having an absent mother and/or father. Have you ever had your parent around physically but they were never been there mentally? Yes, I've witnessed this first-hand amongst loved ones close to me.

More commonly, trying to move forward begins with some type of addiction – whether its alcohol, drugs, sex, or even excessive work behaviors. The parent becomes consumed with something other than being there for their child(ren). Then there are situations where the parent just chooses not to be involved with the child at all or until the parent decides that they are ready. Resentment lingers, arguments are frequent, relationships are damaged, and sometimes they may not speak for long periods of time. The negative effect on the grandkids, personal relationships, and even happiness can suffer from dysfunctional relationships.

She's still your mother… He's still your father. How often do you hear or see this somewhere? Too often if you ask me. We get so caught up in allowing family to treat us any kind of way, well because we give them the "family pass". Wrong is wrong and being mistreated still feels that same no matter who it's coming from. Kids can also become enablers for the parent because they feel that they need to help, but all help should have limits. Everyone must be held accountable for their actions if you want to see different behaviors from them. I'm so big on protecting my peace, that any form of dysfunction or toxicity will be removed from my life. It is okay to love them from afar and pray that they get their lives back on track. However, you must refuse to be pulled down with them.

Break the Cycle

People's stories are real. The hurt and disappointment tends to lessen as time passes, or does it? Sometimes it consumes you and all you feel is resentment, anger, and rejection... the list of emotions is never ending. Then you grow up and you have a choice. A choice to be a victim of your past or to break the cycle of generational curses and not allow your past to define you.

I want to encourage you in this moment to look back into your family history and identify what are the strengths as women and what the weaknesses are as well. It's easy to look at the good things and I agree they help to understand the good family stock that we come from. But it's also necessary to look and say women in my family tend to have issues with obesity, low self-esteem or tend not to make good financial decisions. Don't get stuck but understand looking back allows us to embrace what we need to address and avoid in order to break these generational curses.

In order to love who you are, you cannot hate the experiences that helped shape you. It's easier to store that "baggage" in the closet to avoid opening old wounds. Now comes the real question – how do you heal? You heal the child first to find the adult in you. You forgive, which breaks the cycle and makes you better. I learned that from experience of having to forgive people who were not sorry. I've had to forgive people who I loved and cared deeply about at some point in my life. People who took advantage of my loyalty and pretended to have my best interests. It was one of the toughest parts of growing, but it had to be done. Never be a prisoner of your past!!! Remember it was just a lesson, not a life sentence.

CHAPTER THREE
IS THIS LOVE?

I remember being eighteen years old – I had just graduated from high school and I was ready for the next chapter of my "adult" life. I met a guy right out of high school who became my first love, and I had dreams of us being together forever. I thought I knew everything about love and nobody could tell me anything different. PAUSE! Is it just me or do we all go through this ridiculous phase?

Granted, some young adults do get married straight out of high school and stay together, but it doesn't happen often. PSA: I promise at that age you'll have a lot to learn so don't rush it! Experience has taught me that "teenage love" is just that so don't stress too much about it. Focus on being the best person you can be each day, and whatever is meant will come your way.

I won't be the one to spoil this life lesson for you, but based on the era that we live in I do want to share what love *is not*. Love is not social media relationship goals—that's like comparing your low-lights to someone else's high-lights. It's also not physical, mental, or emotional abuse ladies….

There's a difference between a boy who thinks he might like you and a man who needs your soul next to his. Too often, we allow boys pretending to be men come into our lives and make us question everything that we thought we knew about ourselves. Some of these same boys prey on young and more mature women who lack self-esteem. Low self-esteem is a thinking disorder in which an individual views him/herself as inadequate, unlovable, and/or incompetent.[ ] Nearly 1.5 million high school student's nationwide experience physical abuse from a dating partner in a single year.

One in three adolescents in the U.S. is a victim of physical, sexual, emotional or verbal abuse from a dating partner.[2] Girls and young women between the ages of 16 and 24 experience the highest rate of intimate partner violence — almost triple the national average.[3] Men see these women as easy targets to run over and miss-use which slowly dims her light until it's completely dark. That darkness leads to isolation and 75% of girls with low self-esteem reported engaging in negative activities like cutting, bullying, smoking, drinking, or disordered eating.[4] Then depression follows - About 20% of teens will experience depression before they reach adulthood.[5] Depression in our community is at an all-time high and not enough people are speaking about it. Pay attention to the signs. Young or old, depression does not discriminate.

Check on your loved ones, because a simple "are you okay," can go a long way. We are conditioned to say that we are alright, and having a weak moment is frowned upon. Don't be fooled by how many times a person may *say* they love you. Don't fall in love with potential or what *could* be.

This generation is so pressed for physicality that they forget mentality creates the bond and forms longevity. Take away any sexual relations and you'll come to realize that not many individuals have much to offer. If they're not showing you and making you feel that love, then it's not real. Growing up, you'll learn that love is not a lot of things, but more experience will guide you toward what it truly is. Some say love is indescribable, but I have a few quotes that personally put it into words for me:

Love (n): Defined to me as –

♥ Giving someone the power to destroy you but trusting them not to.

♥ Expressed through sacrifice.

♥ Although defined as a noun, love is also an action word.

♥ A chemistry, a vibe, a spirit, a positive energy.

♥ God is love.

♥ The difference between I like you and I love you: When you like a flower you pluck it, but when you love a flower you water it daily. One who understands this understands life.

My last piece of advice to consider is that love is a decision based on knowing a person. Sometimes we're looking for companionship and we mistake that for a partner.

I've enjoyed the company of people only to find out that we couldn't even build anything together. That was solely my fault because I was so involved with the time spent that I never asked for more. In some cases, we do lead them on by not being clear and discussing expectations up front. Once we get to a point that we want more, it seems as if we switched up on them because the relationship now being tested with what they may call "added pressure". The point is to apply pressure and see who folds and who grows.

This technique quickly separates the men from the boys.

I am learning to own my decisions in relationships and trusting through self-assessment how to avoid self-sabotage. A Queen can adjust when she sees her crown tilting because of her own actions. When you make discoveries about what led you to certain decisions, it's at that point gaps are being bridged through understanding SELF.

It's Not You, It's them

This topic takes me back to a time when I was comparing my relationship status to everyone else's. I knew that I was a down-to-earth person who was easy to talk to, so I often questioned why long term relationships didn't work out in my favor. I went through insecure moments of wondering if I was attractive enough or even worthy. As an adult, I discovered that most guys fear rejection so they tend to go after the easier catch.

I am *the* catch (laughing), but I wouldn't consider myself easy. Any guy who had the pleasure of connecting with me on a deeper level was never supposed to be my end all be all, and I get that now. I was only a pawn used by God to allow them to feel what a real connection, with a real women feels like. They needed to feel that so they could understand that there are levels to everything. I've always exuded a level of confidence that makes me look unapproachable or taken by someone else. I used to dislike this about myself, but with time it became beneficial because it weeded out the guys that weren't *confident enough* to approach me.

A confident man is important to me because it speaks to character and character makes a man. I didn't have anyone to tell me this, so I want to be the voice of reassurance for you - the only reason why guys choose other girls is because they are probably doing a lot more than what you are willing to do. This could happen when you are younger or older.

The immature mind of a guy thinks that he should be with the girl who is known at every party, stays out past curfew, and does whatever she pleases. In comparison, "good girls" are too safe and don't give him the thrill that he is seeking at the time. Then the tables turn – we all grow up and the guy that you may have liked back then has kids with multiple girls who he thought were "popping" back then.

And you'll be sitting there…. A grown, fine, woman who doesn't have time for boys pretending to be men. When they see you, they will instantly remember and regret passing you up because who they thought they *wanted* back then was not who they *needed* to build a life with. As I sit back and reflect, I do it with a smile and grace because I'm so thankful that I didn't end up with what I *thought* I wanted.

CHAPTER FOUR
BE YOUR OWN VALIDATION

After battling the highs and lows of different "situation ships," I was tired of the inconsistencies. I was in my mid-twenties and I had just relinquished a *soul tie,* which took me almost three years by the way. For those of you who don't know, a *soul tie* is an unhealthy, sometimes mentally toxic relationship that stems from sexual relations. They are very powerful and should not be underestimated. I was mentally drained because I had spent so much time trying to fix someone who was not interested in my efforts. I was over guys all together and decided to just focus on what was best for me.

My path for healing consisted of not giving energy to anything or anyone that was not benefiting the progression of my life. During this time, I learned so much more about myself. I learned what my strengths and opportunities were and made that my primary focus. And then I read something that resonated with my soul.

"One morning she woke up different…

She was done with trying to figure out who was with her, against her, or walking down the middle because they didn't have the heart to pick a side. She was done with anything that didn't bring her peace. She realized that opinions were a dime a dozen, validation was for parking, and loyalty wasn't just a word but a *lifestyle*. It was this day that her life changed. Not because of a man, or a job, but because she realized that life is too short to leave the key to her happiness in someone else's pocket". – Author Unknown.

She's began moving differently and the price is going up. She isn't afraid to leave anyone behind. She's authentic and courageous. She's the type of woman most pray for but become intimidated because she knows exactly what she wants. She often needs time to recharge and soak in her solitude.

Why do you doubt yourself, Queen? Don't you know how godly you are? How beautiful you are? Your beauty isn't just looks, it's the way you carry yourself, the way you speak, the way you treat others, the way you live and love. You radiate divine energy. You are a prayer in the flesh. You are fearfully and wonderfully made by God. You heard the lies and quickly embraced that negative perception. Now, with that same energy your faith fuels you to understand that you're better because of you what you experienced. You are enough! Why?? Because you said it. Stop allowing unimportant people to give unwanted opinions about you.

Everything changes when you begin to love yourself. You no longer send out energy of desperation or need to be filled from the outside. You become a powerful source within yourself that attracts better. The more you love who you are, the less you seek validation and approval.

Lastly, being your own validation will require you to have a voice to stand up and say: Soul over body. Energy over matter. Love over fear. Acceptance over judgment. Higher self over the ego. Are you ready for the challenge?

Self-Love = The Best Love

Have you ever thought about all the years of education we have to receive in order to be awarded our high school diploma, yet no one ever taught us how to love ourselves and why it is so important? That was a gap that I closed after I learned that loving yourself brings the glow from the inside out. Self-love can be taught, but not everyone has a teacher.

As a matter of fact, most women battle with self-love because they care so much about what others think of them instead of focusing on what they think of themselves. The goal is to get to a place where you attract people who love, respect, and appreciate your energy. Everything starts with how you feel about yourself. If you respect your mind and body then you begin to silently demand respect from all others, especially men.

You *must* make these guys respect you and make it non-negotiable. It's important that you love yourself as an example of how you expect to be loved. Start feeling worthy, valuable and deserving of receiving the best life has to offer. Be magnetic but selective. Consume a healthier diet so that you feel better and I'm not just talking about food. Your diet is also what you watch, what you listen to, what you read, and the people you allow to hang around you.

Be so completely yourself that everyone else feels safe to be themselves too. Remember only to focus on things that you can control and what you are responsible for. Your words, behavior, efforts, mistakes, ideas, actions, and the consequences of your actions.

I would encourage you to always think before you act to help make smart decisions that can impact your future.

CHAPTER FIVE
GET YOUR S.H.I.T. TOGETHER
(SKINCARE, HAPPINESS, INNER PEACE, TIME)

Ladies…. It's time to set aside some time for YOU. When you look good you feel good, and who doesn't like looking good??

Skin: Understand that your skin is beautiful no matter the color. That melanin that glows is just as bright as the sun. It cannot be replicated because it was given to you from love. Yes, I was there before. Trying to see the beauty within my darker skin on my journey to finding self-love. Be you and own it! Trust me it feels amazing.

We also have to deal with skincare crisis's at some point right?? Acne, period bumps, sex bumps, stress bumps… you name it. Everyone has different skin, so just be sure to have a consistent skincare regimen to keep that stress-free glow.

Happiness: Everyone has a job and that is to be in control of your own happiness. When other things come into your life that should just add to the already full tank that you have. One of the happiest moments in life is when you find the courage to let go of what you can't change. When you need a measuring point, look back at things that you let go and how that lesson helped you.

Inner Peace: A part of being all about you is protecting your peace at all cost. It's ok to cancel a commitment. It's ok to read that text and not respond. It's ok to grow out of a friendship. It's ok to end a toxic relationship without an explanation. It's ok to speak up. It's ok to be you because that's your *superpower.*

Time: The one thing that we all wish we had more of. It controls us daily, but it's up to you to get the most out of it. It's also the one thing that we can never get back. Make sure that those you spend it with are deserving of this precious gift.

You really start to grow when you're happy; mentally, physically, spiritually and emotionally. So baby girl, get your shit together and do you!

Affirm Yourself

I personally use affirmations to help me in my role as a trusted life coach. I treat others the way the way they want to be treated. By treating others the way they want to be treated, my own personal fulfillment grows. I give respect and provide service. I show love, care, compassion, and consideration. I help others feel appreciated. I let others know they are important, that they matter, and that they are valuable.

By valuing others, my confidence increases. I believe in myself and when I fail, I learn. My failures are temporary because my perseverance is permanent. I push forward at all times because I know I can succeed.

As I continually believe in myself, my tenacity expands. I have high standards. I do not let mediocrity enter my life. I am honest. I do not apologize for striving for excellence. My quality of life is a reflection of my high standards. I rise and lift others with me. By living up to my personal high standards, my poise has become undeniable. Lastly, I trust my gut. I value my intuition, since it is based on my subconscious mind and conscious mind working in harmony. I know what is true, and I know what I want to be true. I have faith in my inner voice. As I trust myself, my self-assurance is completely declared. The goal when practicing positive affirmations is to increase your level of confidence. You need to believe what you are saying will manifest into your life.

Confidence is Silent, Insecurities Speak Loud

Confidence is not: "They will like me." Confidence is: "I'll be fine if they don't!" Nothing is more dangerous than a beautiful woman who is focused and unimpressed. A woman who is not looking for a come up but building one. This type of women doesn't speak much, but commands the attention of a room when she walks in. This type of woman can also be intimidating to less secure women, because she has much more to offer without even saying a word.

Many women including myself have been pre-judged by other women, young and old, because we carry ourselves with a sense of confidence and choose not to follow the "latest trend." Remember, some of us are just protecting our peace and being happy.

Now that we've brought awareness to the situation, let's be the difference in this world full of *look at me girls* and be a *come with me girl.* Be that girl who roots for the other girls, tells a stranger her hair looks amazing, and encourages other women to believe in themselves. Let's not attempt to tear her down because she feels highly of herself, but let's encourage her to shine her light even brighter and all my other ladies get in formation!

"You have the power to change perception, to inspire and empower, and to show people how to embrace their complications, and see the flaws, and the true beauty and strength that's inside all of us" – Beyoncé.

Who run the world? GIRLS.

Social Media Impacts

Everything is at the swipe of the thumb. This is what we've come to know as the generation of social media, but it has its pros and cons like anything else. It's great for marketing purposes, staying connected with friends and family, and reaching people near and far to bring awareness. It could also be used in a negative manner where it consumes your mind, makes you counterproductive, and you easily lose track of time. I fell into a trap where I became addicted to reading things that did not mentally challenge me. Reading most of what I saw on social media began to mess with my energy and peace of mind. I had to train my mind differently and learn that everything that I saw was not for me to read. I also became more self-aware with how much time I spent on my phone and set some limits for my sanity.

Another well-known issue on social media is the amount of cyber bullying that occurs. Cyber bullying is at an all-time high and although we can't change the world, one small step in the right direction is a start. Events that are destructive or tragic such as fights, car accidents, abuse, or even fatalities are highlighted in hopes to go "viral" for the world to see. When this happens no one is thinking about how the victims or their families may be impacted, but more about how many "views" and "likes" their post will receive. It's very sad to say that this generation of individuals laugh and makes jokes about people's real pain. We tell others to speak their truth and own it – maybe they are recovering from something and feel good about their accomplishments. Or maybe, they just want to speak about something positive that's going on in their life. Sometimes, I read other people's comments just to see how many comments were encouraging and how many comments stem from misery and loneliness.

Other times I would practice restraining and purposely avoid reading the content. There is a lack of compassion and understanding because we don't know what the next person is going through. It's estimated that about 88% of teens have seen someone be mean or cruel to another person on social media.[6] Too many young kids and teens are deciding their own fate due to the self-hate that they've allowed others to instill in them. Too many people are focused on the wrong things. If everyone took that negative energy and used it to make something positive happen in *their* life, there would be less cyber bullies and more of us working together. Don't be a victim, or the person responsible for causing someone such pain.

Believe it or not – most people are not as successful as social media makes them look or as pretty as those filters make them seem. The only healthy and worthwhile comparison you should make is you yesterday versus you today.

Social media has taught me that perception is not always reality, to block out negativity, to be a leader, and to think for myself. Do what you like and not because someone made something look "cool" for a short period of time. Remember this shall too fade…

CHAPTER SIX
CIRCLE GOT SMALLER
(Everybody Can't Go)

"I am at a place in life where peace is a priority. I deliberately avoid certain people and situations to protect my mental, emotional, and spiritual state". – Author Unknown

Experience has taught me that who you choose to associate yourself with becomes a reflection of you. If you surround yourself with people who are negative, jealous, promiscuous, or just complacent you can inherit those type of behaviors. Even if you don't inherit the traits they display, you become known to associate with them. Another common pitfall is when people who have been friends for a long period of time feel obligated to maintain a friendship that they know expired years ago.

Maybe you grew apart from that person, you no longer have the same interests, or the relationship is toxic and unhealthy for you.

Whatever the reason is, choose happiness over history and let it go like Elsa! People will notice the change in your attitude towards them, but won't notice their behavior that made you change. Don't allow others to guilt trip you into holding on to one-sided relationships and always give people enough space so that you can see what they'd rather do. Resisting change is what creates energy blockages. Accept what is showing up for you right now so that you can flow with it.

Are you prepared for the shift and elevation?

Throughout my growth and my career, I've been blessed with some strong ladies in my corner.

Now, I haven't known these ladies all my life, and most of them I didn't even attend high school with, but when you grow new friendships evolve to match the new you. Everyone is so quick to say "no new friends," but creating and adjusting your circle is healthy and necessary. You are the CEO of your life. You must hire, fire, and promote accordingly.

If you don't have a best friend, a real one, then get you one because mine is the best! You need someone that you know you can trust with everything. You also need a strong circle of women to rally around you when you feel at your lowest. You need your girls to tell you when you're wrong and to help you get it right.

There was a point in my life when I had all of these made up problems in my head. I sought advice from someone who, at the time, I didn't know anything about. The fact that she was comfortable in her element drew me in to say more to her.

I spilled out everything to her about my relationship or lack thereof, my career goals, and not knowing what to do during this chapter of my life. I was constantly worried about the next part of my life without realizing that I was right in the middle of what I used to look forward to. Her timely response was, "Shenaé, you don't have any problems and you're not supposed to have all of the answers right now." A simple sentence that held so much meaning to me then and now.

What she meant was, everything that I thought was a problem wasn't and would sort itself out when the time was right.

Aries women lack patience and it drives me crazy sometimes, but I am learning to manage it better. I also learned to pick my battles throughout life based on some advice that another close friend gave me. My assertiveness makes me so quick to respond when I don't agree with something.

She helped me find balance on when to speak and when to just listen whether I agree or not. From there, bonds were formed and to this day I may still reach out to these ladies if I need some advice. It was with these particular experiences that I learned that we women need that support because without it you could start to feel alone. With it, I feel invincible—like I can do all things through my girls rhythmically chanting, "Aye!" to strengthen me. Surround yourself with people who think like you and who have dreams and aspirations such as yourself.

Listen to their ideas, go to their events, buy what they're selling, share their posts and PUSH THEM. Celebrate in their victories and remind them of their importance after their failures. The goal should be to make memories with the people who are important to you, and to do it every chance you get.

Vibes Don't Lie...

Let your vibe be a product of your heart and not your environment. **Read that again.** That gut feeling that we call our intuition and learning to trust it – why is this so hard for some women? We ask for a sign and when we receive ten, we are still looking for something else. As your frequency upgrades and your intuition becomes stronger, you will notice how much other people's energy actually affects you. The more spiritually attuned you become, the more sensitive you are to energy in general. When you become more focused on your energy, people will think that you are being distant, but in reality you are just gravitating towards the vibes that suit you. Don't ignore your intuition. It's simply data processed too fast for your conscious mind to comprehend.

Keep your circles pure, sacred and small. Trust the signs and the red flags. It could be a friendship, relationship, business partnership, etc. – when something doesn't seem right then most of the time it's not.

Don't allow anyone to make you question what you already know, trust me I've been there before. A part of growth is trusting the seeds that you're planting within yourself will manifest. If you don't believe in you, the universe won't either. Once you start believing in yourself then you'll reach the next chapter of your life – THE LEVEL UP.

CHAPTER SEVEN
ALLOW ME TO RE-INTRODUCE MYSELF

Don't assume you know me by what you heard. I grow

daily, and your messenger may have outdated information.

I sat down with the universe and told her that I wanted to grow. I told her to use me as a vessel, so she made me uncomfortable. She stripped me of everything that I knew – made me learn how to be silent, how to let go, how to move on, how to stand my ground, how to be more understanding, how to fight, how to survive, how to be more assertive, more loving, and less naïve. She told me to take everything that I learned during this process and share it with others.

During the year of 2018, I spent a lot of time trying to find myself because I was in a *comfort zone* where I felt safe and in control as a performance coach. Although I had many thoughts during this time about a career change, I didn't know where to start because the *fear zone* had set in due to a lack of confidence and I was worried about other peoples' opinions. At the beginning of 2019, I had a different mindset. It was my *learning zone*. I read books to acquire more knowledge, dealt with challenges as they arose, and extended my comfort zone. I mustered up some confidence and self-motivation to find what I was truly passionate about and to make that a part of my life. This transition lead me to my *growth zone* where I was on a mission to find purpose, set new goals, and live my dreams.

Discovering My Passion and Going After it

I walk like I already got it, because God told me it's mine.

I sat at the dining room table rambling on and on to my mom about how I wanted to help people. I had a list of things that I knew meant a lot to me, but I didn't know where to go next… A few topics on my list were:

- To encourage and support
- Helping others reach their full potential
- Giving compliments that help motivate
- Being inspired by *true* love
- A feeling of excitement when I see others succeeding, especially women

At that moment with the help of my supportive mother, I knew that I wanted to be a life coach and someday a best-selling author.

Most people don't know exactly what a life coach is so I want to bring awareness to this fast-growing career field. A life coach is a personal, motivating-supportive *partner* who listens to what one is trying to accomplish and help them figure out a plan of action, unlike a therapist.

Coaching is different from therapy because it is hyper-focused on who you are now and who you want to evolve into for the betterment of your life.

- My Life Coaching Philosophy: *I believe that coaching is an ongoing professional relationship that helps people produce results in their lives, careers, businesses, and organizations.*
- *Through coaching, clients deepen their learning, improve their performance, and enhance their quality of life.*

Transitioning from a performance coach to a certified life coach allowed me to combine my expertise in coaching and developing with something more personal and aligned with my passion which is to push self-motivated individuals to be the best version of themselves. We are all a work in progress, so I must also be the best version of myself because it's important to lead by example.

How Can I Help and What to Expect

My *signature coaching program* is geared toward girls and women who struggle with balancing the highs and lows of life along with maintaining self-care. I also work with female athletes to improve time management between their demanding careers and personal life. I will help them push through any adversities or hardships that may otherwise stunt their performance. They will understand the importance of decreasing stress levels to increase happiness and productivity.

Being clear with client expectations is a must so that you understand what you signed up for, literally. Here are the steps I take to help my clients become successful:

C – Capture Details
O – Optimize Solutions
A – Assist with Action Plans
C – Continue Support
H – Hold you Accountable

Success takes hard work and hard work always pays off. During your coaching sessions I will capture the intricate details of your situation. I then gather that information and start to optimize some personalized solutions just for you. The process is always collaborative, so as my client we work together to develop the best plan of action to get you going in the right direction. As your partner, I am there with you every step of the way to help you to see your full potential and to cheer you on. Lastly, this journey of taking charge of your life won't be easy, but the effort that you put out will be the results that you get back.

I will seek to understand any barriers you may be facing, but ultimately hold you accountable for your actions.

Another benefit of hiring a life coach, such as myself, is to help you develop better relationships in your life. Seeking someone to help you progress in life allows you to take ownership and learn to hold yourself accountable even after your sessions have ended. The benefit of having someone celebrate your accomplishments builds confidence.

Confidence builds character, and then you will become an inspiration to those around you to make changes as well. It becomes a positive, domino affect toward greatness! If you decide that you are not ready to hire someone right now, that's okay. Many life coaches share great content on their websites for you to use in your own life. In this book I share some of my own personal experiences and provide a few *self-help* steps to get you going in the right direction.

However, for more details and insight visit my website at

www.CoachShenae.com

Some personal advice I would offer before taking the initiative to hire a coach would be to mentally prepare yourself, so when challenges arise you won't be tempted to quit on yourself. My motto is to start where you are and grow to where you want to be. My passion for being a life coach is how I am living my life. My goals are what I choose to create in my life.

CHAPTER EIGHT
DON'T BE PERFECT BE REAL

Life is not about being rich, popular, highly educated or perfect. It's about being real, humble and kind. Courage is being yourself every day in a world that tells you to be someone else. I want you to visualize your highest self and start confidently showing up as her every day. In reality, other people liking you is a bonus. You liking yourself is the real prize. Take a deep breath, look in the mirror and remember who you are.

As women we are not perfect and shouldn't claim to be. We have insecurities, we get jealous, overthink, and may have trust issues from past lessons. Why they ask? Because we are human. We are also amazing in many ways too. We have big hearts, we are naturally nurturing, and we are strong beyond anything else – never forget that.

I think it's important to incorporate some morals and values into your life. I also wanted to touch on some clear expectations in the chapter on behalf of all women. ***Say it louder for the people in the back!***

- Every action does not require a reaction. For the non-believers: Karma is real and patient – what you put out you will get back. A strong women doesn't seek revenge, but moves on and lets karma do her dirty work.

- Move in silence and be exclusive. You don't have to be everywhere, with just anyone. Leave some mystery to your life. Thank me later.

- Sometimes you will be too much for someone and you will have to let them go back to what they are comfortable with.

- Stay motivated. This isn't a race. It's a life decision.

Let's be real we are NOT always the HERO in the story but in some cases we were the villain. Choosing to cope through retaliation, and using anger as a crutch for our explosive attitudes. I can't say it enough it's not what people do to you that determines your quality of life, but rather how you respond to tragedy is what's REAL.

Moving in silence is understanding that people don't have to be updated about the progress that's happening beneath the soil. It's like a tree, no one ever celebrates the root despite it being the strongest part of the tree.

Focus on your core (being a root) and as you grow in silence your roots will begin to sprout up and the time for recognition will come.

Again being too much for someone is not being arrogant but understanding that we were not always REAL or forthcoming with people because we didn't consider where we were going at the interim. Sad but it's a real place when you decide you want more and without notice your pursuit of purpose can cause them to leave you. I've had more relationships dissolve because I kept going and not because we fell out over some major issue.

Being too much speaks of goals being realized and dreams pursued assuming everyone you have great affection for will be with you when you finish your journey. You will have seasonal relationships and long term relationships but the ones that stay were contributors to you becoming enough and even the people who left helped you to grow into who you are today. Everyone has value and we learn from the Good, Bad and the Ugly things we had to go through.

To every person that feels like your social life is severely lacking and you're starting to feel like the process is robbing you of enjoyment. In this moment let me confirm you're having the pains that come with striving for better and you're one step closer to becoming. What hurt you made you consider options for change and that's motivation. Having bad credit taught you the value of good credit, even something as serious like divorce helped you to at least discover what you didn't want. These things being motivation are based on perception and perspective.

How do you see it? It's within you to rise above anything that you're facing. Somewhere there's a young girl who has no idea of the strength that's in her but because she refuses to quit she'll become that lawyer, doctor, or media-mogul. We are the bridges to the next generation and the transparency we show to the youth matters if they are to become great. Looking into the eyes of a little girl who thinks she can do anything but fail is a flame I refuse to dim.

CHAPTER NINE
STRAIGHT UP NO CHASER

Women are some of the most undervalued individuals. We have to fight for a place, for our opinions to be heard, for fair pay, and to be appreciated for all that we do. As a woman, I exercise my right to assertively speak up. Whether it's in the workplace or at in the comforts of your own home, don't be a pushover who will allow others to mistreat you. Instead, say what you mean and mean what you say. Learn self-control by speaking when needed, and listening and observing when appropriate. You don't have to try to be the smartest person in the room, but be the most aware. Never be afraid to question something that doesn't make sense to you.

Anyone can draw attention to themselves through being loud, but when you're clear and precise you can never be denied what belongs to you. Many of us have to negotiate at the table of life and business but the master key is listening to your environment. Every room has a sound and if you pay attention you'll begin to understand how different people function and the system they operate in. Speaking too soon, can expose your ideas in a way that minimizes your voice. Consider what you bring to the table but also consider those who've been at the table longer than you. Everyday decisions are being made to keep valuable information from you, but when we come in unassuming we learn how to make impact through our listening ears. You were not created to live on barely make it street, but as a Queen you have the power to decide what your family and children should enjoy.

You Got My Attention, Now What Are You Going to Do with It?

Side effects of focus include less drama, more accomplishments, more abundance, and better results. However, there are many distractions when you least expect it. Is it just me, or do ex-boyfriends get some type of "Spidey-sense" when you are happy and living your life? Or is this someone new that has been trying to get your attention for some time now? Maybe it's family drama or just something that is requiring more attention than you want to give? We have all been there before, but it's in these moments where you let it be known that you're about your business so that becomes your full-time focus. Be selfish with you without regrets and remember if a woman holds the power to create life, she holds the power to create the life she wants. Let that be your daily motivation.

CHAPTER TEN
THE PRESSURES THAT MAKE DIAMONDS

The societal pressures that women have to endure can be a heavy burden to carry. Have you ever felt like you're getting older and you're not in a relationship and you *should* be? Or you're in a relationship and everyone is asking you about marriage? Better yet, you're married but decided to travel and enjoy your marriage before having children? Society would call women like this selfish. I've always wondered who made up these rules for us. Some women have found balance with these pressures and others are still finding their way.

I have firsthand experience with feeling pressured by other people, but more importantly feeling the pressure that I put on myself. Before I reached this level of maturity, I remember being about twenty years old when I created an unrealistic timeline based on the order my life was *supposed* to go in. At twenty five I was *supposed* to be in a long-term committed relationship and by thirty

I was *supposed* to be married with at least 1-2 kids. When the relationship timeframe came and went, I felt devastated. I didn't like this feeling of disappointment, so I knew that I had to change the way I set expectations for myself and monitor the expectations that I allowed others to impose on me.

If I've ever told you about my past, it's not because I want you to feel sorry for me, but because I want you to understand why I am who I am and why I move the way I move.

I look at things so differently now. It's very likely that I won't be married with kids by the time my 30th birthday arrives, and guess what? I'm at peace with that. It's no longer a race for me, but a steady progression of growing and becoming a better person every day. God has not sent my husband or made me a mother yet because it's not my time. I learned to take that energy that I was putting out and give it back to myself and as a result this book was birthed.

I pray that these words touch someone who needs to hear them and help that person relinquish any pressures that's holding them back from living up to their full potential. Be patient, your time is coming. In the meantime, continue to shine like the diamond that you are and remain UNAPOLOGETICALLY YOU!

CHAPTER ELEVEN
TOTAL COST OF OWNERSHIP

➢ Own who you are
➢ Own your failures
➢ Own your mistakes
➢ Own your success
➢ Own the next chapter of your life

When was the last time your wrote down a goal and made consistent steps toward reaching that goal? In this chapter we get honest with ourselves and reflect.

Sometimes our biggest road block is the person staring back at us. Now it's your turn. Please take the mini accountability test to jump start your next move. The purpose of this short test is to help you put your attention on the important necessities to propel your life forward.

1. What is your ***greatest*** weakness? What have you done in the last 30 days to help turn this into a strength?

    _____

    _____

2. What are your best practices for ***time management***?

    _____

    _____

3. What was the most ***recent bad decision*** that you made? How has your thought process evolved since then?

    _____

    _____

4. When was the last time you evaluated your ***work ethic***? If this is an area opportunity for you, what's your plan moving forward?

    _____

    _____

5. How will you help *young girls* who come after you?

_____

_____

Thank you for your participation!

Now look back on your answers – understand your strengths and opportunities listed. Now use this as leverage to start your plan of action! You got this ☺

For more insight on how to jump start the next chapter of your life – visit my website to schedule a free consultation!

www.coachshenae.com

Closing: Happiness Looks Good on You!

You are growing and glowing, beautiful. So, you finally decided to start believing in yourself and now you are living your best life! How does it feel to know that all of your hard work is paying off?

It's feels amazing, you are evolving, and the things that you prayed for became the things that you have. Now it's time to put you first. You spend your days helping people because that's what you enjoy doing, but this "ME time" should be different. Get your hair done, get cute, and be the alarm clock to wake everyone up who is sleeping on you. Be in control of your life and don't wait for someone to tell you when to make the next move. Stay ready so that you don't have to get ready.

Don't spend years doing something that you hate doing because you can later resent yourself for it. Instead, take advantage of the knowledge and experience that you gain along your journey and allow it to build you. If you don't already know what you're passionate about, start paying more attention to the things that make you smile throughout the day. This process allows you to become more aligned with following your heart.

I know this may sound like something you've heard before, but my own personal experiences have allowed me to connect with myself in many different ways as I continue to grow.

Once you find what you love to do – do it every day until it no longer feels like work. Remember, no matter how successful you get at what you do, always send the elevator back down for the up and coming Queens.

ABOUT THE AUTHOR

Shenaé Pitts was born and raised in Pontiac, Michigan. Growing up in a small city made her realize early on that she wanted to stand out, be different and make a positive impact on those around her. Being a natural born leader allowed her to take a stance on topics that she felt strongly about, and work to be a part of the solution. She turned her 6+ years of expertise in coaching and developing into a career. She became a Certified Life Coach to assist young girls and women manifest the life they want to live. Shenaé chose this particular career because she understands the struggle of balancing life and making time for yourself. With this, her very own life coaching business idea was birthed, putting her in full control of her purpose. As an entrepreneur she plans to learn the ropes and share her knowledge to help others be successful as well. Why? Because there's enough opportunity for everyone to win. This is just the beginning, so please continue to follow her successful journey as she works to change the lives of others.

Shenaé Pitts
Can be contacted for Book signings, and
Workshops by visiting one of the contact methods
below for more details.

Coach Shenaé
8225 Allen Rd Suite 1059
Allen Park, MI 48101
CoachShenae@Yahoo.com
www.CoachShenae.com

Points of Reference: (See Below)

1. NEUMAN, M.D., FREDRIC. "LOW SELF-ESTEEM." PSYCHOLOGY TODAY. ACCESSED MARCH 3, 2014. HTTP://WWW.PSYCHOLOGYTODAY.COM/BLOG/FIGHTING-FEAR/201304/LOW-SELF-ESTEEM.

2. DAVIS, ANTOINETTE, MPH. 2008. INTERPERSONAL AND PHYSICAL DATING VIOLENCE AMONG TEENS. THE NATIONAL COUNCIL ON CRIME AND DELINQUENCY FOCUS. AVAILABLE AT HTTP://WWW.NCCD-CRC.ORG/NCCD/PUBS/2008_FOCUS_TEEN_DATING_VIOLENCE.PDF.

3. CENTERS FOR DISEASE CONTROL AND PREVENTION, "PHYSICAL DATING VIOLENCE AMONG HIGH SCHOOL STUDENTS—UNITED STATES, 2003," *MORBIDITY AND MORTALITY WEEKLY REPORT*, MAY 19, 2006, VOL. 55, NO. 19.

4. PR Newswire Association LLC. . "New National Report Reveals the High Price of Low Self-Esteem." Dove Self-Esteem Fund. Assessed March 2, 2014. http://www.prnewswire.com/news-releases/new-national-report-reveals-the-high-price-of-low-self-esteem-65355592.html.

5. BORCHARD, THERESE J.. "WHY ARE SO MANY TEENS DEPRESSED?." PSYCHCENTRAL. ACCESSED MARCH 3, 2014. HTTP://PSYCHCENTRAL.COM/BLOG/ARCHIVES/2010/03/04/WHY-ARE-SO-MANY-TEENS-DEPRESSED/.

6. HTTPS://WWW.GUARDCHILD.COM/SOCIAL-MEDIA-STATISTICS-2/